Boundary Breakers

Remarkable People

Library of Congress Cataloging-in-Publication Data

Parham, Jerrill.
    Boundary breakers : remarkable people / by Jerrill Parham.
        p. cm. -- (Shockwave)
    Includes index.
    ISBN-10: 0-531-17752-1 (lib. bdg.)
    ISBN-13: 978-0-531-17752-5 (lib. bdg.)
    ISBN-10: 0-531-15488-2 (pbk.)
    ISBN-13: 978-0-531-15488-5 (pbk.)

1. Biography--Juvenile literature. 2. Heroes--Biography--Juvenile literature.
I. Title. II. Series.

    CT107.P248 2008
    920--dc22

2007012224

Published in 2008 by Children's Press, an imprint of Scholastic Inc.,
557 Broadway, New York, New York 10012
www.scholastic.com

SCHOLASTIC, CHILDREN'S PRESS, and associated logos are trademarks
and/or registered trademarks of Scholastic Inc.

08 09 10 11 12 13 14 15 16 17
10 9 8 7 6 5 4 3 2 1

Printed in China through Colorcraft Ltd., Hong Kong

Author: Jerrill Parham
Educational Consultant: Ian Morrison
Editor: Frances Chan
Designer: Anne Luo
Photo Researcher: Jamshed Mistry

Photographs by: Anne Luo (Hammurabi portrait, p. 10); **Big Stock Photo** (p. 5); **Carol Hsu**
(sign language class, p. 13); **Courtesy of Gallaudet University** (statue, p. 12); **Courtesy of Lynn
Morawski and Janna Morawski** (Loretta Claiborne, pp. 32–33); **G. F. Jones & Son photograph,
Sheppard Collection, Canterbury Museum** (Kate Sheppard, p. 19); **Getty Images** (p. 8; Chico
Mendes, p. 9; protestors, p. 24; Chico Mendes, p. 26); **The Granger Collection, New York**
(Eleanor Roosevelt with the Declaration of Human Rights, p. 21); **The Green Belt Movement/
www.greenbeltmovement.org** (pp. 28–29); **Jennifer and Brian Lupton** (teenagers, pp. 32-33);
Photolibrary (p. 11; pp. 22–23); **The Queens Borough Public Library, Long Island Division,
Latimer Family Papers Collection** (Lewis Latimer, p. 17); **The Royal New Zealand Foundation
of the Blind** (woman at keyboard, keyboard close-up, p. 15); **Stock.Xchng** (p. 34); **Sustainable
South Bronx/www.ssbx.org** (cover; pp. 30–31); **Tranz/Corbis** (p. 3; p. 7; Thomas Gallaudet,
Aung San Suu Kyi, p. 9; Thomas Gallaudet, p. 12; Marlee Matlin, p. 13; p. 14; Helen Keller,
p. 15; Frederick Douglass, p. 17; Lucy Stone; suffragists march, pp. 18–19; p. 20; Eleanor
Roosevelt with friends, p. 21; Aung San Suu Kyi, p. 24; p. 25; rubber tapper, p. 26; p. 27)

All illustrations and other photographs © Weldon Owen Education Inc.

Boundary Breakers

Remarkable People

Jerrill Parham

children's press®

An imprint of Scholastic Inc.
NEW YORK • TORONTO • LONDON • AUCKLAND • SYDNEY
MEXICO CITY • NEW DELHI • HONG KONG
DANBURY, CONNECTICUT

CHECK THESE OUT!

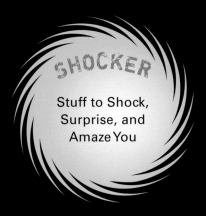

SHOCKER

Stuff to Shock, Surprise, and Amaze You

Quick Recaps and Notable Notes

Word Stunners and Other Oddities

The Heads-Up on Expert Reading

Links to More Information

CONTENTS

activist a person who takes action to support a cause

boundary something that indicates a limit or extent

campaign (*kam PAYN*) to work and inform others in order to reach a certain goal

conservation (*kon sur VAY shuhn*) the protection of the environment, plants, and animals

grassroots involving the local people

humanitarian (*hyoo man uh TEHR ee uhn*) a person who is devoted to caring for others and to improving their lives

justice (*JUHSS tiss*) the quality of being good and fair

nonviolent protest an action or demonstration to bring about change, which does not hurt people or damage property

For additional vocabulary, see Glossary on page 34.

The -*ist* in the word *activist* indicates a person who is involved in a job, profession, or activity. Other similar words include *artist*, *dentist*, and *geologist*.

Eleanor Roosevelt serves
food to unemployed women
and their children in 1932.

Who is a **boundary** breaker? It's someone who sees a need for change and makes it happen. Just because something has been done in a certain way for years is no reason to assume that there is no better way. Sometimes people find themselves with few rights and little freedom. Laws may be unfair. People often have a hard time fighting for themselves. But an extraordinary person may come along and break through barriers. Societies and laws have been changed because of extraordinary reformers.

Students at the Alabama Institute for the Deaf and Blind learn to communicate using sign language and Braille. This is thanks to the boundary-breaking work of Thomas Hopkins Gallaudet and of Louis Braille.

The boundary breakers in this book have done remarkable things to help humankind. Some have risked their lives so that **immigrants**, women, and people with disabilities can have more freedom and opportunities. Other boundary breakers have worked to improve the natural world. Their ideas have made us care more for the **environment**. Like people, the earth also needs protection.

Some Boundary Breakers From Around the World

Eleanor Roosevelt

Lucy Stone

Louis Braille

Thomas Hopkins Gallaudet

Hammurabi

France

Babylonia (Iraq)

U.S.A.

India

Kenya

Frederick Douglass

Brazil

Myanmar (Burma)

Mohandas Gandhi

Majora Carter

Aung San Suu Kyi

Chico Mendes

Wangari Muta Maathai

> If he breaks another man's bone, his bone shall be broken.

Lawmaker, Lawgiver

Hammurabi (about 1810 B.C.–1750 B.C.)

Long ago, a king named Hammurabi ruled Babylonia (modern-day Iraq). He made the country into a great **empire**. He built temples and canals. He fought many wars. Hammurabi was a tough ruler. But he believed in **justice** for his people. He was one of the first kings in ancient times to write out a set of laws. The 282 laws were carved into a stone pillar. They listed specific penalties for specific acts against society. We call these laws the Code of Hammurabi.

Hammurabi

> The speech bubble makes me feel as if the person the story is about is talking directly to me. It helps me understand what was most important to that person. I'll look out for more speech bubbles as I read the rest of the book.

A close-up of the ancient writing on the stone pillar

The Code lists crimes and their punishments. It tells how to settle arguments. The laws seem strict by today's standards. However, writing down laws for the information of the public was an important step in setting up a justice system. Now all governments have written laws.

SHOCKER

The Code of Hammurabi says that if a slave hit another person, his or her ear would be cut off. If a person was caught stealing, he or she would be killed.

The stone pillar on which the Code of Hammurabi is written is more than seven feet high. It was discovered in 1901. It now stands in the Louvre Museum in Paris, France.

Strange Laws

According to local laws, the following actions were once illegal in some parts of the United States:

• going to a movie sooner than four hours after eating garlic

• taking a lion to a movie

• putting pennies into your ear

• walking down a street while carrying bees in your hat

• snoring before locking all bedroom windows

• riding a bike in a swimming pool

• teasing a skunk

• letting a donkey sleep in a bathtub, a horse eat a fire hydrant, or a chicken cross the road (That's no joke!)

• carrying ice cream in your pocket while flying or waiting to board a plane

Master of Signs

What shall this universal language be? Is there already one ... which demands neither types nor paper?

Thomas Hopkins Gallaudet

Thomas Hopkins Gallaudet (1787–1851)

Thomas Gallaudet was a preacher. One day, he met a deaf girl named Alice. Although she was nine years old, she could not communicate. She could not go to school. No one in the United States knew how to teach people who couldn't hear. Gallaudet decided that this situation must change.

Gallaudet traveled to England. He visited a school that taught lipreading. However, the teachers refused to show him their methods! Gallaudet was finally taught a sign language at a school in France. He went home and started his own school. Alice was one of his pupils. Gallaudet used the French signs and developed American Sign Language. He proved that people with hearing disabilities can be educated successfully.

SHOCKER

In the past, deaf people were kept from public life. They were put in homes away from their families and were not educated.

In 1864, Gallaudet's son Edward started the world's first college for hearing-impaired students. The campus is in Washington, D.C. It is now called Gallaudet University. It features a statue of Thomas Gallaudet and Alice.

A B C D E F G H I J K L M N O P Q R S T U V W X Y Z

Many countries have their own versions of sign language. For example, there are American Sign Language and British Sign Language. Most hearing-impaired students also wear hearing aids to help them communicate.

Signs of Achievement

Marlee Matlin started acting at seven years old. When she was twenty, she won the Academy Award for Best Actress in *Children of a Lesser God*. She is the youngest actress and the only deaf one to win this award. In 2007, she performed at the Super Bowl in Florida. She signed the words to *The Star-Spangled Banner* in American Sign Language.

Code Maker

> We must be treated as equals. Communication is the way we can bring this about.

Louis Braille

Louis Braille (1809–1852)

Louis Braille became blind as a result of an accident when he was three years old. At a regular French school, he found it difficult to learn everything just by listening. Then Louis went to a special school. It was a school for boys who were blind. Learning was still slow.

One day, a man introduced the school to a system. It was called "night writing." It was originally invented so that soldiers could pass secret instructions during wartime. The code used twelve raised dots and dashes in different combinations to make letters. It was hard to follow. So fifteen-year-old Louis invented his own code. He used six raised dots. He also developed codes to write math and music. The system he invented was named after him. In 1829, the first book in Braille was published. However, Braille was not taught until many years after Louis Braille's death. Today, Braille is the standard form of reading and writing for people who are visually impaired.

The Braille code has been adapted into many languages. There is Braille in Chinese, Japanese, and Arabic.

A B C D E F G H I J K

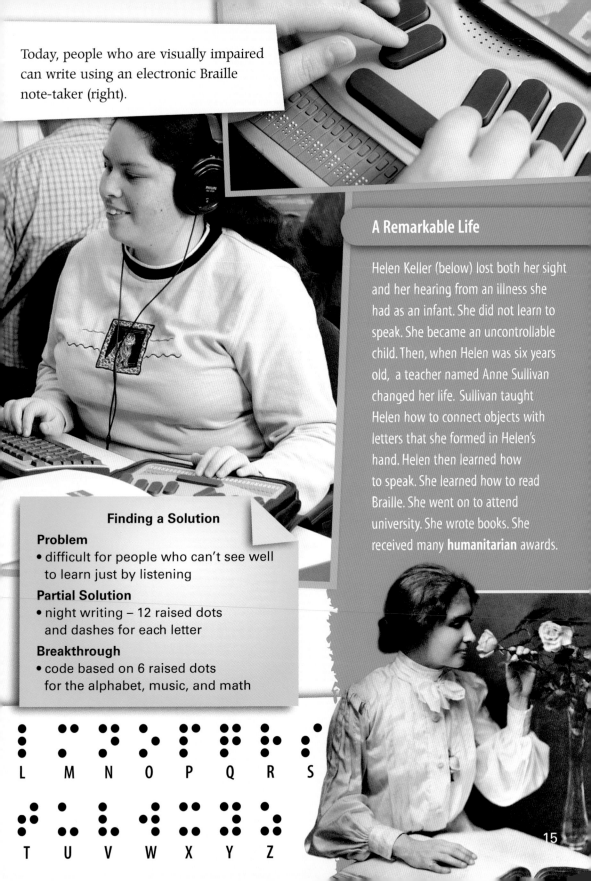

Today, people who are visually impaired can write using an electronic Braille note-taker (right).

A Remarkable Life

Helen Keller (below) lost both her sight and her hearing from an illness she had as an infant. She did not learn to speak. She became an uncontrollable child. Then, when Helen was six years old, a teacher named Anne Sullivan changed her life. Sullivan taught Helen how to connect objects with letters that she formed in Helen's hand. Helen then learned how to speak. She learned how to read Braille. She went on to attend university. She wrote books. She received many **humanitarian** awards.

Finding a Solution

Problem
• difficult for people who can't see well to learn just by listening

Partial Solution
• night writing – 12 raised dots and dashes for each letter

Breakthrough
• code based on 6 raised dots for the alphabet, music, and math

L M N O P Q R S

T U V W X Y Z

To suppress
free speech is
a double wrong.
It violates the
rights of the
hearer as well
as those of
the speaker.

Brilliant Speaker

Frederick Douglass (1818–1895)

Frederick Douglass was born into slavery. He lived on a farm in eastern Maryland. As a boy, he was separated from his mother. He was sent to live with a family in Baltimore. The mistress of the house gave him reading lessons, until her husband forbade it. From then on, Frederick taught himself how to read and write.

In 1838, Douglass escaped from slavery. He disguised himself as a sailor on a train heading north. Then he began to tell his story. Douglass wanted freedom and voting rights for all African Americans. He gave **inspiring** speeches for many years. He even gave advice to Presidents Abraham Lincoln and Andrew Johnson.

Frederick Douglass

I wasn't quite sure what *forbade* meant. As I continued to read, it became clear that the word is a form of "forbid." It's really great how most new words can be figured out without having to look them up.

Did You Know?

President Lincoln abolished slavery in 1863. However, laws in some states made it nearly impossible for many African Americans to vote. The situation finally changed with the Voting Rights Act of 1965.

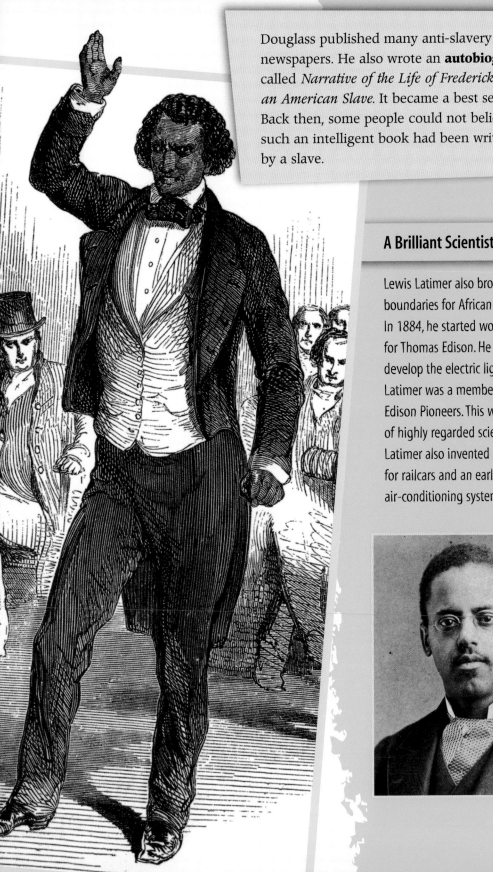

Douglass published many anti-slavery newspapers. He also wrote an **autobiography** called *Narrative of the Life of Frederick Douglass, an American Slave*. It became a best seller. Back then, some people could not believe that such an intelligent book had been written by a slave.

A Brilliant Scientist

Lewis Latimer also broke boundaries for African Americans. In 1884, he started working for Thomas Edison. He helped develop the electric lightbulb. Latimer was a member of the Edison Pioneers. This was a team of highly regarded scientists. Latimer also invented a toilet for railcars and an early air-conditioning system.

My name is my identity and must not be lost.

Campaigner

Lucy Stone (1818–1893)

Lucy Stone broke boundaries at a young age. Her father would not pay for her education. So she saved up her own money for college. She became the first woman from Massachusetts to earn a bachelor's degree. Stone was also the first American woman to keep her own name when she married. She did not share the belief that men should own slaves, wives, or children.

Lucy Stone

Lucy Stone
- saved her money to go to college
- was first woman from Massachusetts to get a bachelor's degree
- campaigned for women's right to vote

Did You Know?

The Nineteenth Amendment to the U.S. Constitution was passed in 1920. It finally gave American women the right to vote. Stone did not live to see it.

Stone **campaigned** for women to have the right to vote. This is known as women's suffrage. In 1869, she helped form the American Woman Suffrage Association. The members were called suffragists. Because women were not allowed to vote, Stone refused to pay taxes. The tax collector took all her household goods to sell. However, Stone's friends bought them back.

World First

Kate Sheppard was one of the world's leading women suffragists. This famous New Zealand woman was an intelligent and powerful speaker. She **rallied** huge support for the women's movement. In 1893, New Zealand was the first country in the world to allow women to vote.

CITY WOMEN

VOTE AT ALL.

In the early 1900s, suffragists in the United States and all over the world held many protest marches.

19

First Lady

Eleanor Roosevelt (1884–1962)

Eleanor Roosevelt was the wife of U.S. President Franklin D. Roosevelt. She did things that no First Lady had done before. She traveled around the country to see how the poor lived. She wrote her opinions in a daily newspaper column. She gave lectures and radio and television interviews on human rights.

Eleanor Roosevelt visited many people in need. On Christmas Day in 1947, she gave out presents at the Wiltwyck School for Boys, in New York state.

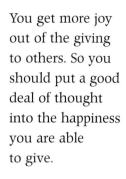

Eleanor Roosevelt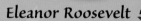

Did You Know?

The Universal Declaration of Human Rights was presented on December 10, 1948. Since then, this date has been known as Human Rights Day.

After the president died, Mrs. Roosevelt served as head of the **United Nations** (UN) Human Rights Commission. She helped write the UN's Declaration of Human Rights. She received many humanitarian awards for her work. There is also an Eleanor Roosevelt Award for Human Rights. This award honors other outstanding American human rights **activists**.

Eleanor Roosevelt liked to invite people to her home to talk about current issues.

First Lady is an interesting term. In this case, *first* means "most important" (married to the most important person in the country – the president). If a woman becomes president, and she is married, I wonder if her husband will become the *First Man*?

Know Your Rights

Eleanor Roosevelt was very proud of the UN's Universal Declaration of Human Rights. It's a long list of rights deserved by every human being. The list includes:

- the right to freedom of speech

- the right to freedom from slavery or torture

- the right to travel and live wherever you want

- the right to be considered innocent until proven guilty in a court of law

- the right to own property

- the right to equal pay for equal work

- the right to a free education

- the right to receive help if you are sick, unemployed, or disabled

Mohandas Gandhi

Peaceful Protestor

Mohandas Gandhi (1869–1948)

Mohandas Gandhi was born in India. India had a strict social system. This divided people according to class, or caste. People in the poorer castes had little hope of changing their position. Gandhi was born into a wealthy caste. However, he was aware of many injustices. At that time, India was part of the British Empire. It was ruled by Great Britain. Indians were considered inferior citizens in their own country. Because he was from a wealthy family, Gandhi was able to study in England. He went to London to study law. There he faced **discrimination** because of the color of his skin.

Gandhi began his professional life as a lawyer in South Africa. Like India, South Africa was under British rule. In South Africa, Gandhi faced discrimination as an immigrant from India. In 1906, he started a **nonviolent protest** against the government.

The word *caste* is taken from the Latin word *castus*, meaning "pure or chaste." In societies that have a caste system, people are grouped according to family ties, occupation, or wealth.

For seven years, Gandhi and many others were often beaten and jailed. Finally, the government agreed to give more rights to immigrants.

The British mistreatment of Indians in India continued. Gandhi returned home and became the leader of the Indian nationalist movement. Thousands joined him in peaceful protests. One of Gandhi's nonviolent acts was to **fast** for extended periods. He endured many years of imprisonment for his actions. In 1947, India became an independent country. The world saw that nonviolent mass protest could bring about change.

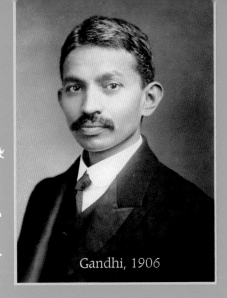

Gandhi, 1906

The Great Soul

Gandhi gave away all his clothes and possessions. He lived simply, like the poor. That earned him more respect, even from his enemies. The people called him Mahatma (Great Soul) and Bapu (Father).

In 1930, Gandhi led a 240-mile march to the sea. He wanted to protest the British tax on salt. The march swelled to thousands of people over the course of 23 days. At the coast, the protestors symbolically made their own salt by evaporating seawater. They did not pay any tax. This march sparked more nonviolent protests across India. Gandhi was eventually arrested. But the situation in India received worldwide attention.

SHOCKER

In 1893, Gandhi was forced to get off a train in India even though he had a first-class ticket. Another time, a stagecoach driver beat him for not giving his seat to a white person.

Freedom Fighter

Aung San Suu Kyi (1945–)

Aung San Suu Kyi (*Oun San Soo Chee*) symbolizes the **democracy** movement in Myanmar, also known as Burma. Myanmar is one of the poorest countries in the world. It is under strict military rule. Its people have few human rights. Protestors against the government are often imprisoned, beaten, or killed. Aung San Suu Kyi has spent about 20 years protesting the **antidemocratic regime** that rules her country. She says she has been inspired by the life of Gandhi.

Aung San Suu Kyi

People all over the world organize nonviolent demonstrations to demand freedom for Aung San Suu Kyi.

Of course! I thought the author had forgotten to finish writing the dates beside Aung San Suu Kyi's name. Now I understand that since there is only a date of birth, she must still be alive.

In 1988, Aung San Suu Kyi formed the National League for Democracy. She called for an election of a new government. During the campaign, she was put under house arrest without charge or trial. She was not allowed to leave her home. Her party easily won the election. Aung San Suu Kyi should have been made prime minister. However, the military rulers refused to step down. Despite worldwide protests, Aung San Suu Kyi remains under house arrest to this day.

Aung San Suu Kyi makes a speech from behind the gate of her house.

Party for Freedom

The United States Campaign for Burma organizes "Arrest Yourself" house parties around the world. Participants keep themselves under house arrest for 24 hours. They invite their friends over to learn more about Aung San Suu Kyi and the situation in Myanmar.

Did You Know?

In 1991, Aung San Suu Kyi was awarded the Nobel Peace Prize. She was still under house arrest. Her sons accepted her prize for her.

Rain-Forest Man

Chico Mendes (1944–1988)

> At first, I thought I was fighting to save rubber trees. Then I thought I was fighting to save the Amazon rain forest. Now I realize I am fighting for humanity.

Chico Mendes tapped liquid from rubber trees in the Amazon rain forest in Brazil. People had been doing this for hundreds of years without damaging the trees. Then cattle ranchers and mining companies began clearing the forest. The rubber tappers lost income. Animals lost their homes. The newcomers were making money but damaging the rain forest. That is when Chico Mendes went into action.

Rubber tappers cut the trees on an angle. The liquid inside drips down. It collects in a bucket.

Chico Mendes

Did You Know?

Every year, more than 9,000 square miles of Amazon rain forest are destroyed. That's an area bigger than the state of Vermont!

Mendes founded the National Council of Rubber Tappers. The group wanted to create **sustainable** forest reserves. Mendes even spoke to the United Nations General Assembly. His campaign had some success. International banks gave less money for road construction in the rain forest. Mendes became a hero to many people. He won awards for his work as an environmental activist. However, the rain forest is still disappearing. Future generations must continue to campaign to protect the forest.

Preserving the Reserves

Today, there are 25 sustainable forest reserves in Brazil. The reserves are protected by the government. Traditional communities continue to manage them. The local people harvest rubber, fruits, nuts, oil, and plant medicines from the reserves.

SHOCKER

In 1988, Mendes was murdered in his home. The two ranchers who killed him were sentenced to only 19 years in prison.

Rain forests are chopped down for timber, or cleared by burning. Thousands of plant and animal species are lost each year.

Tree Champion

> I was inspired to plant trees to help meet the basic needs of **rural** women.

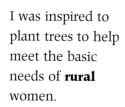

Wangari Muta Maathai

Wangari Muta Maathai (1940 –   )

Like the forests in Brazil, the forests in Kenya, East Africa, are also disappearing. The trees are being chopped down for firewood and building materials. The land is being used for new settlements, crops, and grazing animals. However, **deforestation** has caused water sources to dry up. The soil has become **infertile**. Rural people cannot make a living from the land. Kenya is at risk of becoming a desert like the Sahara, in North Africa. Wangari Maathai knew that positive action was needed to improve people's lives.

Members of the Green Belt Movement plant trees on an eroding hillside.

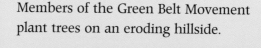

Forests

Brazil
- chopped and burned
- replaced by ranches
- animals lost homes
- people lost income

Kenya
- chopped down
- water sources dried up
- soil became infertile

In 1977, Maathai started the **grassroots** Green Belt Movement. The group plants trees all over Kenya to prevent soil **erosion**. Members are able to earn money by raising tree seedlings in nurseries. They then sell them to farmers for planting. The organization also educates people on the importance of **biodiversity** and **conservation**. Maathai has gained much respect in a society that is traditionally dominated by men. In 2004, she became the first woman from Africa to win the Nobel Peace Prize.

Trees for Life

The simple act of planting a tree gives many benefits. Maathai says, "Trees stop soil erosion. This leads to water conservation and increased rainfall. Trees provide fuel, and material for building and fencing. They offer fruits, **fodder**, shade, and beauty."

Did You Know?

Since 1997, the Green Belt Movement has planted more than 20 million trees all over Kenya.

In 2006, Maathai published an autobiography called *Unbowed.* She celebrated the launch of her book by planting a tree.

29

Urban Greenie

Majora Carter (1966–   )

Majora Carter grew up in the South Bronx. It is one of the poorest communities in New York City. The area is surrounded by rivers and bays. However, for many years, residents have had almost no waterfront access. Forty percent of the city's garbage is dumped in the South Bronx. There are power plants, sewage treatment plants, and heavy traffic. These are sources of serious pollution. The rate of asthma in the South Bronx is one of the highest in the United States. Until very recently, there have been few parks and very little community spirit. Majora Carter is working to change all that.

Majora Carter

Carter wants to turn wasted concrete spaces, such as the one below, into green areas. These areas will beautify the neighborhood. They will provide a meeting place for residents to enjoy (right).

SHOCKER

Diesel trucks pollute the air as they haul garbage, meats, and produce to the South Bronx. They drive in and out of the borough 60,000 times a week!

In 2001, Carter founded Sustainable South Bronx (SSB). Its first project was the South Bronx Greenway. This is a tree-lined path for people and cyclists along the waterfront. Now more residents can enjoy the river views and fresh air. Another SSB proposal is to turn an underused expressway into an area for parks and housing. SSB installs green roofs, too. It also runs courses in river conservation and **horticulture**. Carter's organization is improving the landscape of the South Bronx. The result is a safer, greener community.

What Is a Green Roof?

A green roof is covered in a layer of soil and growing plants. There are many benefits of a green roof.

• Plants give off oxygen from respiration.

• Plants absorb heat, so buildings are cooler. Therefore, less money is spent on air-conditioning.

• Green roofs soak up rainwater, so less water runs into city drains.

• Roof plants can produce food.

• Green roofs are beneficial for birds and insects. The plants provide a place for them to live. The animals help to pollinate the plants. Some insects help to decompose plant material.

SSB is helping to develop the South Bronx Eco-Industrial Park. At the park, waste will be recycled into new products. These include glass, compost, paper, and rubber products. Barges and rail transportation will replace diesel trucks.

... American Loretta Claiborne was born with a mild **intellectual disability**. Other kids teased her. Running was Loretta's escape from anger. She trained hard and became a great marathon runner. She won many medals at the **Special Olympics**. Now Loretta is a spokesperson for that organization and for the rights of people with intellectual disabilities.

WHAT DO YOU THINK?

Can everyone be a boundary breaker?

PRO

Everyone can push his or her personal boundaries. We can all set a good example for others. I think everyone can do something to help the community. It's important to have goals so you can improve your life. Then you are in a better position to help others.

Loretta speaks about her life to many different groups. She encourages people to overcome their personal boundaries. Loretta is not just a champion athlete. She also has a black belt in karate and speaks four languages, including sign language. She is the only person with an intellectual disability to have been awarded **honorary doctorates** from two universities.

CON

I think some people are born to be leaders. These people have the big ideas. They have a natural ability to inspire others. But you don't have to be a leader or win awards to make positive changes in your life or the lives of the people around you.

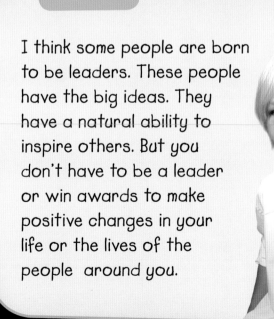

GLOSSARY

antidemocratic against democracy

autobiography a history of a person's life written by that person

biodiversity (*bye oh duh VUR suh tee*) the variety of different plants and animals living in an area

deforestation the permanent removal of trees in a forest

democracy (*di MOK ruh see*) a way of governing a country in which the people choose their leaders in elections

discrimination (*diss krim i NAY shuhn*) prejudice or unjust treatment based on differences in age, race, or gender

empire a group of countries or territories ruled by the same governing power

environment the natural surroundings in a place, including the plants and animals, landforms, bodies of water, and climate

erosion the wearing away of land by water, ice, or wind

fast to go for a long time without eating

fodder food for livestock

honorary doctorate an academic degree awarded to someone who has made a valuable contribution to society in a specialist field

horticulture the science of growing plants, including flowers, fruits, and vegetables

immigrant (*IM i gruhnt*) a person who comes from abroad to live permanently in a country

infertile not able to grow crops

inspire to move to action

intellectual disability learning difficulty

rally to bring together

regime (*reh JEEM*) a government that rules people for a specific period of time

rural to do with the countryside; not urban

Special Olympics a sporting competition for people with intellectual disabilities

Rural

sustainable (*suh STAIN uh buhl*) able to be continued without long-term negative impact on the environment

United Nations an international organization of countries that promotes world peace

FIND OUT MORE

BOOKS

Endres, Hollie J. *Scientists Try, Try Again*. Scholastic Inc., 2008.

Jeffrey, Laura S. *All About Braille: Reading by Touch*. Enslow Publishers, 2004.

Kamma, Anne and Johnson, Pamela. *If You Lived When There Was Slavery in America*. Scholastic, 2004.

Kent, Deborah. *American Sign Language*. Franklin Watts, 2003.

Krull, Kathleen. *Lives of Extraordinary Women*. Harcourt Children's Books, 2000.

Pastan, Amy. *Gandhi*. DK Publishing, 2006.

WEB SITES

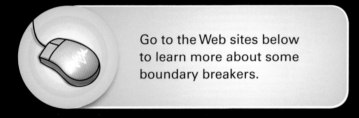

Go to the Web sites below to learn more about some boundary breakers.

www.lorettaclaiborne.com

www.ssbx.org

www.greenbeltmovement.org

www.afb.org/braillebug/louis_braille_bio.asp

www.mkgandhi.org/students/introduction.htm

INDEX

ABOUT THE AUTHOR

Jerrill Parham has written and edited dozens of books for young people. She believes that people of all ages, far away and close to home, are doing something amazing every day, and they don't all make the news or history books. Now Jerrill enjoys researching how her own family has been breaking boundaries they faced through hundreds of years.